It's Easy To Play Gilbert & Sullivan.

Wise Publications
London/New York/Sydney/Tokyo/Cologne

Whitwams Music Ltd.
70 High Street
Winchester SO23 9DE
Tel. (0962) 65253

Exclusive distributors:
Music Sales Limited
78 Newman Street, London W1P 3LA, England.
Music Sales Pty. Limited
27 Clarendon Street, Artarmon, Sydney, NSW 2064, Australia.
Music Sales GmbH
Kolner Strasse 199, 5000 Cologne 90, West Germany.
Music Sales Corporation
4-26-22 Jingumae, Shibuya-ku, Tokyo 150, Japan.
Music Sales Corporation
33 West 60th Street, New York, N.Y. 10023, USA.

This book © Copyright 1979 by
Wise Publications
ISBN 0.86001-629.3
Order No. AM24225

Compiled and arranged by
Cyril Watters

Music Sales complete catalogue lists thousands
of titles and is free from your local music
book shop, or direct from Music Sales Limited.
Please send 15p in stamps for postage to
Music Sales Limited, 78 Newman Street, London W1P 3LA.

Printed in England by
West Central Printing Co. Limited, London and Suffolk.

Sing "Hey To You, Good-Day To You"

from Patience

By Gilbert and Sullivan
Arranged by Cyril Watters

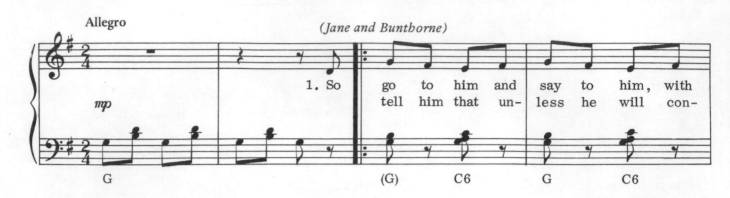

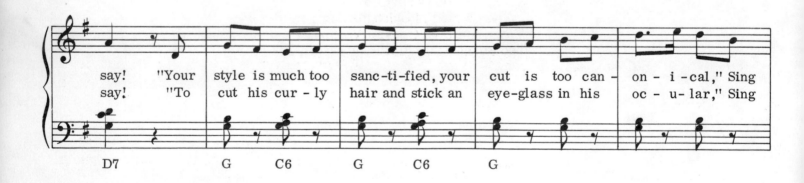

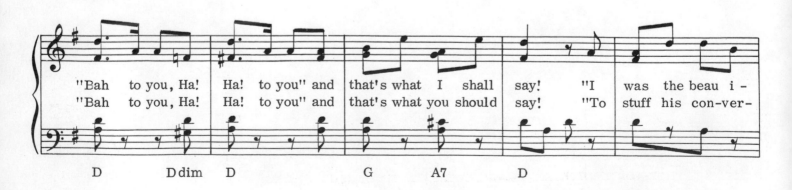

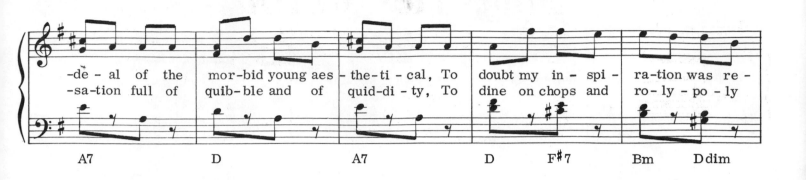

A7 D A7 D F#7 Bm Ddim

-de - al of the / mor-bid young aes - the-ti - cal, To / doubt my in - spi - ra-tion was re -
-sa-tion full of / quib-ble and of / quid-di - ty, To / dine on chops and / ro-ly - po-ly

A D F#7 Bm Ddim D A

-gard-ed as he - / re - ti-cal, Un- / til you cut me / out with your pla - / ci - di - ty e-
pud-ding with a - / vi - di-ty, He'd / bet - ter clear a - / way with all con - / ve - ni-ent ra -

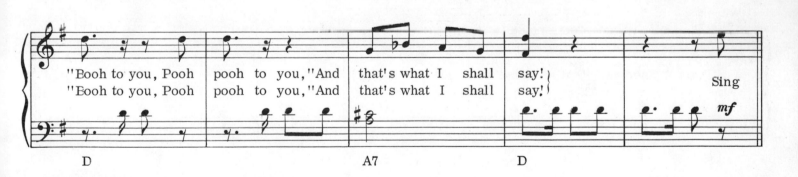

D Cm7 Fb7 D7

-me-ti-cal." Sing / "Booh to you, Pooh / pooh to you" And / that's what I shall / say! Sing
-pi-di-ty." Sing / "Hey to you, Good / -day to you" And / that's what you should / say! Sing

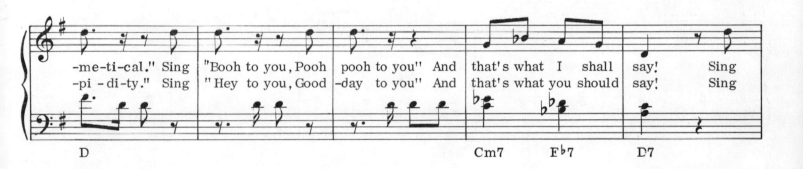

D A7 D

"Booh to you, Pooh / pooh to you,"And / that's what I shall / say! } Sing
"Booh to you, Pooh / pooh to you,"And / that's what I shall / say! } mf

G D9

"Hey to you, Good- / day to you" Sing / "Bah to you, Ha! / Ha! to you" Sing / "Booh to you, Pooh

pooh to you," And that's what you should say! Sing "Hey to you, Good-day to you," Sing

G

"Bah to you, Ha! Ha! to you," Sing "Booh to you" And that's what you should say! "Bah,

D9   G

Booh, Bah Booh," And that's what I shall say! "Bah, Booh, Bah,

C   G   C   G   Am7   D7   G   C   G

1

Booh," And that's what I shall say! 2. I'll

C   G   C   D7   G

2

I shall say!

D7   G

Little Buttercup

from H.M.S. Pinafore

By Gilbert and Sullivan
Arranged by Cyril Watters

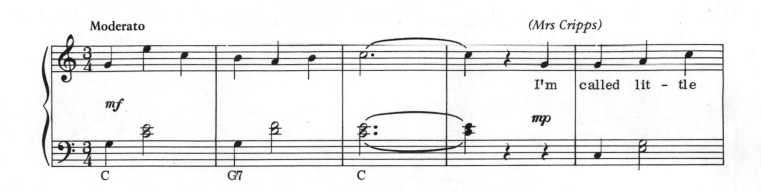

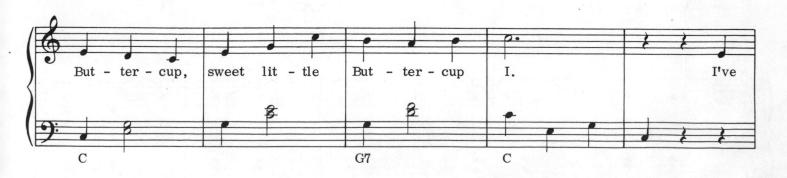

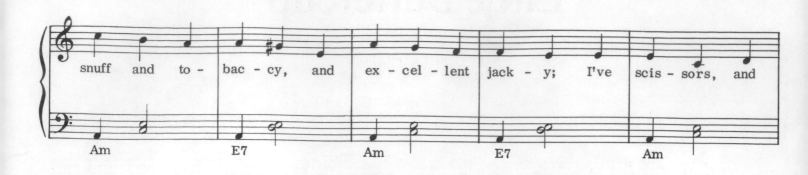

snuff and to - bac - cy, and ex - cel - lent jack - y; I've scis - sors, and

Am | E7 | Am | E7 | Am

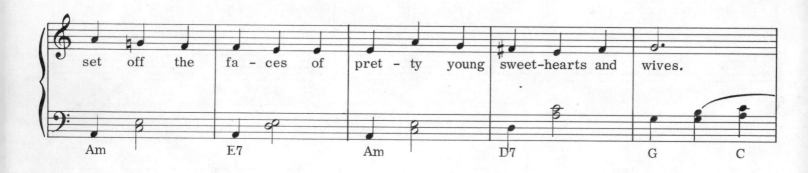

watch - es, and knives. I've rib - bons and la - ces to

E Am E7 Am E Am E7

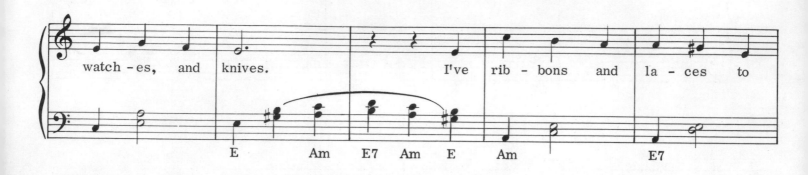

set off the fa - ces of pret - ty young sweet-hearts and wives.

Am | E7 | Am | D7 | G C

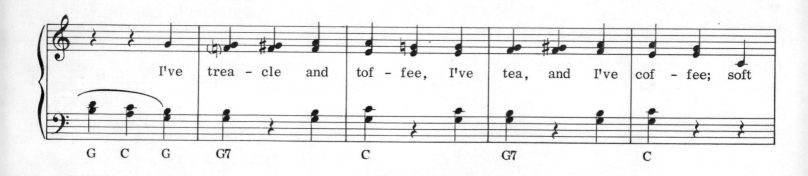

I've trea - cle and tof - fee, I've tea, and I've cof - fee; soft

G C G G7 C G7 C

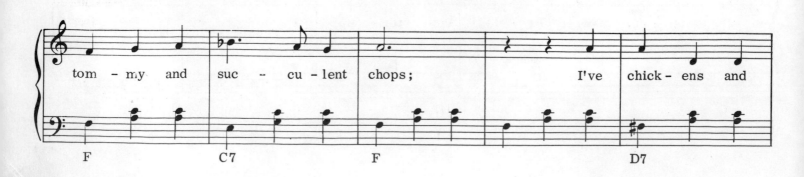

tom - my and suc - cu - lent chops; I've chick - ens and

F C7 F D7

Let's Give Three Cheers

from H.M.S. Pinafore

By Gilbert and Sullivan
Arranged by Cyril Watters

Moderato
(Chorus)

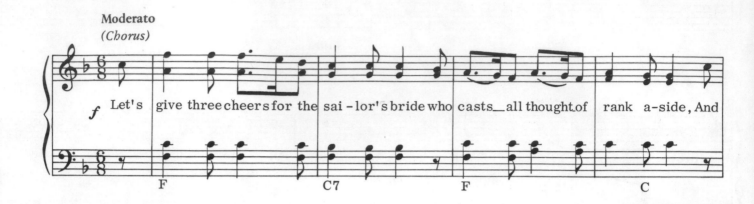

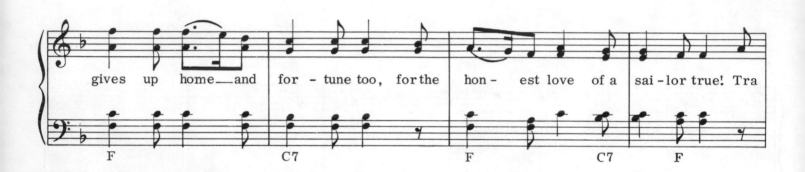

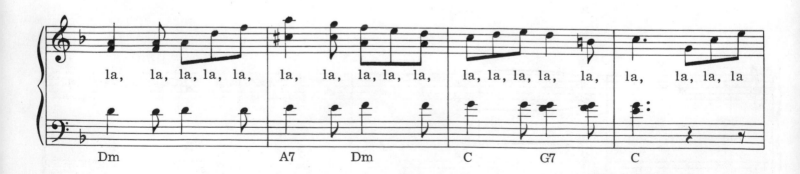

la, la, la, la, la, la, la, la, la, la, la, la, la, la, la, la, la, la, la, la,

G7   C6   G   C6

la, la, la, la, la, la, la, la, la, la, la, la, la, la, la, la. Let's

G7   C6   G   C

give three cheers for the sai-lor's bride, who casts__ all thought __ of rank a-side, And

F   C7   F   C

gives up home __ and for-tune too for the hon — est love of a sai - lor true!

F   C7   F   C7   F

F   C7   F

The Sun Whose Rays

from The Mikado

By Gilbert and Sullivan
Arranged by Cyril Watters

Down a 4th!

Very Slow

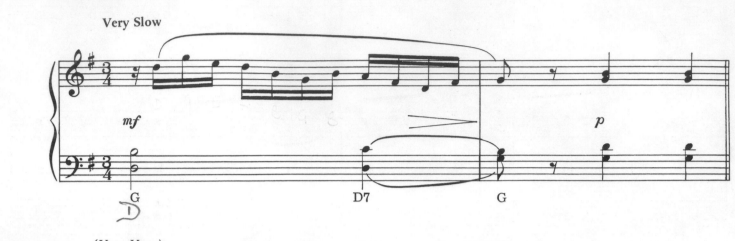

(Yum Yum)

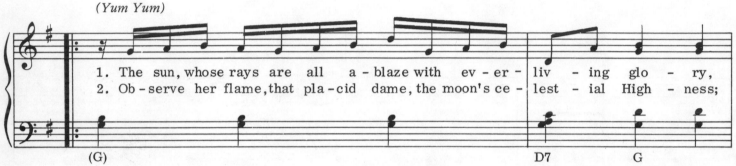

1. The sun, whose rays are all a-blaze with ev-er-liv-ing glo-ry,
2. Ob-serve her flame, that pla-cid dame, the moon's ce-lest-ial High-ness;

Does not de-ny his ma-jes-ty, he scorns to tell a sto-ry!
There's not a trace up-on her face of dif-fi-dence or shy-ness:

He don't ex-claim "I blush for shame, so kind-ly be in-dul-gent,"
She bor-rows light that thro' the night, man-kind may all ac-claim her!

Gavotte

from The Gondoliers

By Gilbert and Sullivan
Arranged by Cyril Watters

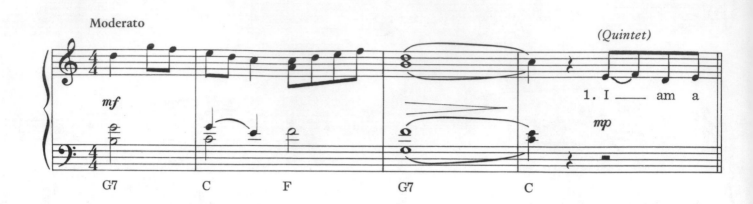

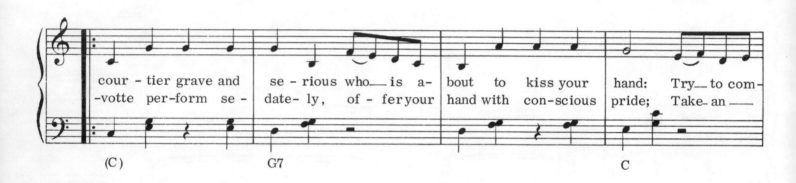

14

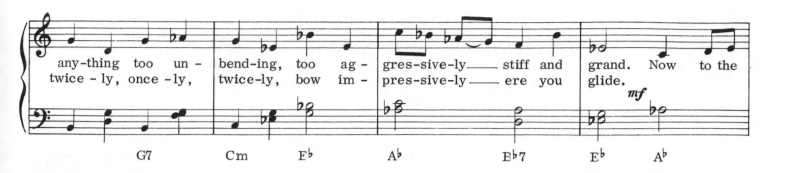

any-thing too un - | bend-ing, too ag - | gres-sive-ly___ stiff and | grand. Now to the
twice-ly, once -ly, | twice-ly, bow im - | pres-sive-ly___ ere you | glide. *mf*

G7   Cm   E♭   A♭   E♭7   E♭   A♭

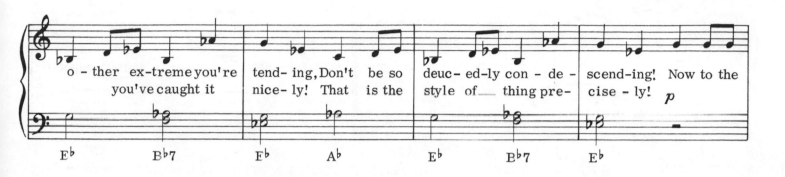

o - ther ex-treme you're | tend- ing, Don't be so | deuc- ed-ly con - de - | scend-ing! Now to the
        you've caught it | nice - ly! That   is the | style of__ thing pre - | cise - ly! *p*

E♭   B♭7   E♭   A♭   E♭   B♭7   E♭

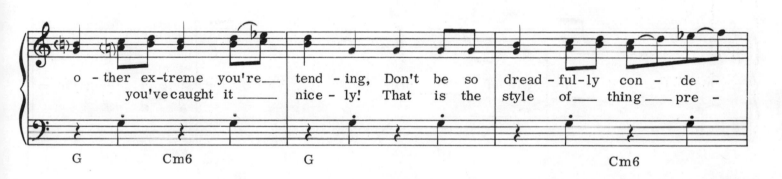

o - ther ex-treme you're__ | tend - ing, Don't be so | dread - ful-ly con - de -
        you've caught it __ | nice - ly! That   is the | style of__ thing __ pre -

G   Cm6   G   Cm6

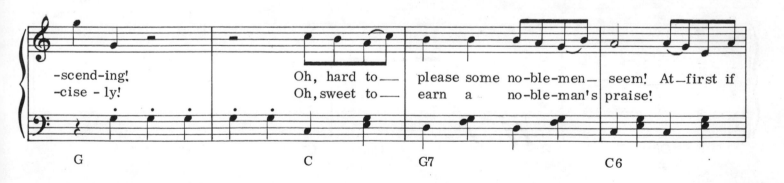

-scend-ing! | Oh, hard to __ | please some no-ble-men__ | seem! At__first if
-cise - ly! | Oh, sweet to __ | earn a   no-ble-man's | praise!

G   C   G7   C6

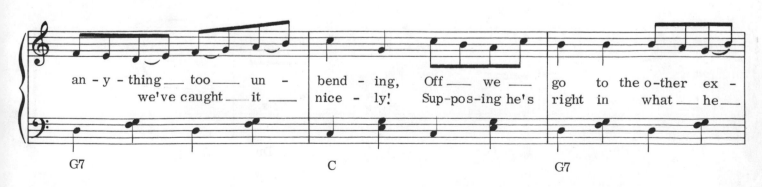

an - y - thing __ too __ un - | bend - ing, Off __ we __ | go to the o - ther ex -
        we've caught __ it __ | nice - ly! Sup-pos-ing he's | right in   what __ he __

G7   C   G7

The Flowers That Bloom In The Spring

from The Mikado

By Gilbert and Sullivan
Arranged by Cyril Watters

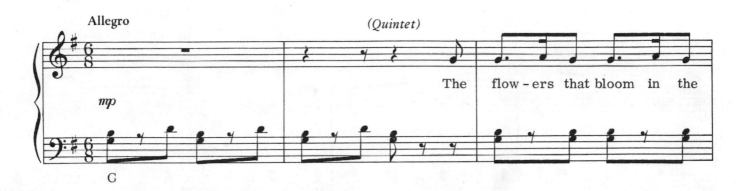

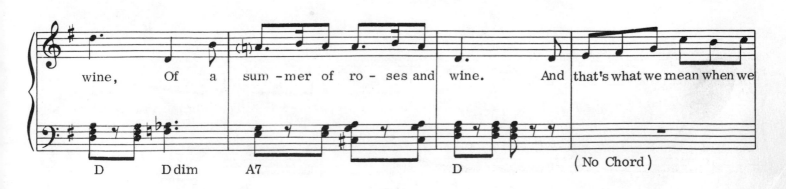

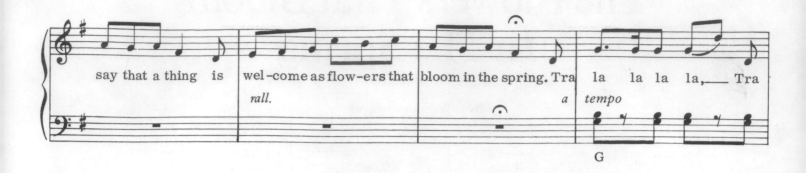

say that a thing is wel—come as flow—ers that bloom in the spring. Tra la la la la,___ Tra

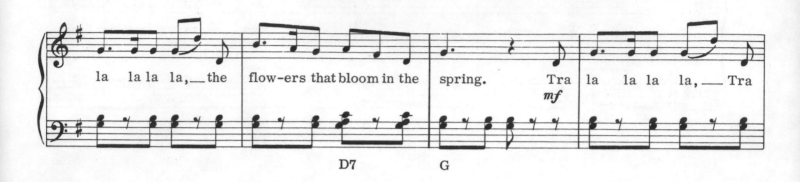

la la la la,___ the flow—ers that bloom in the spring. Tra la la la la,___ Tra

la la la la,___ Tra la la la la la! The

flow—ers that bloom in the spring, Tra la, have no—thing to do with the case. I've

got to take un—der my wing, Tra la, a most un—at—tract—ive old thing, Tra la, with a

car - i - ca - ture of a face, with a car - i - ca - ture of a face. And

A7   D   Ddim   A7   D

that's what I mean when I say, or I sing, "Oh bo-ther the flow-ers that bloom in the spring." Tra

rall.   *a tempo*

(No Chord)

la la la la, — Tra la la la la, — "Oh bo-ther the flow-ers of spring. Tra

G   D7   G

mf

la la la la, — Tra la la la la, — Tra la la la la la! —

f

Fm   C   D7   G

Em   C   D7   G

When Britain Really Ruled The Waves

from Iolanthe

By Gilbert and Sullivan
Arranged by Cyril Watters

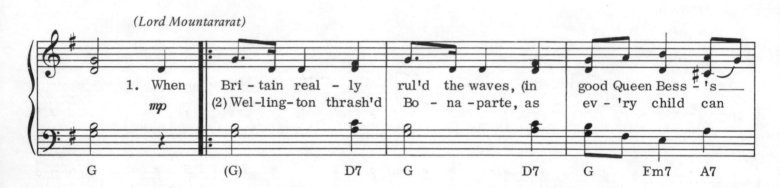

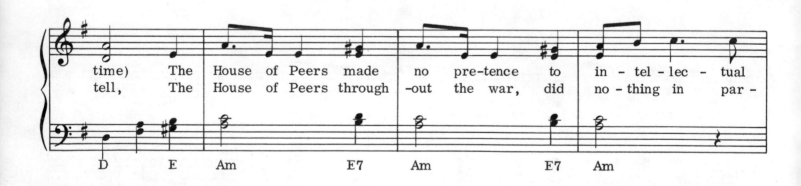

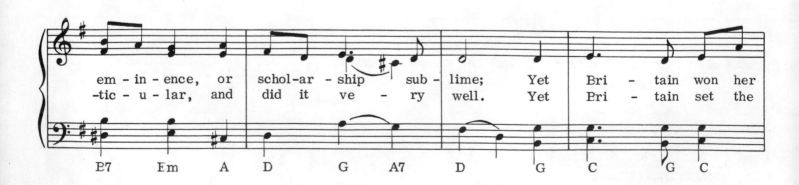

proud-est bays in good Queen Bess-'s glo - rious days! Yet Bri - tain won her
world a blaze in good King George's glo - rious days! Yet Bri - tain set the

D   Fm   C   D   G   C   G   Am7

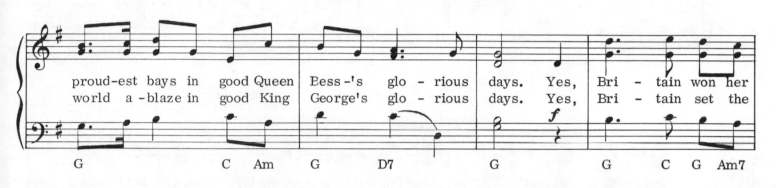

proud-est bays in good Queen Bess-'s glo - rious days. Yes, Bri - tain won her
world a -blaze in good King George's glo - rious days. Yes, Bri - tain set the

G   C   Am   G   D7   G   G   C   G   Am7

1.2.   **3.**

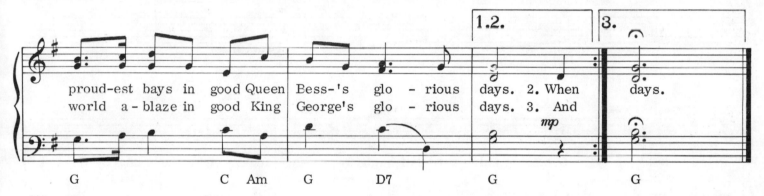

proud-est bays in good Queen Bess-'s glo - rious days. 2. When | days.
world a -blaze in good King George's glo - rious days. 3. And

G   C   Am   G   D7   G   G

3. And while the House of Peers withholds
    Its legislative hand,
    And noble statesmen do not itch
    To interfere with matters which
    They do not understand;
    As bright will shine Great Britain's rays
    As in King George's glorious days!

When A Wooer Goes A-Wooing

from The Yeoman Of The Guard

By Gilbert and Sullivan
Arranged by Cyril Watters

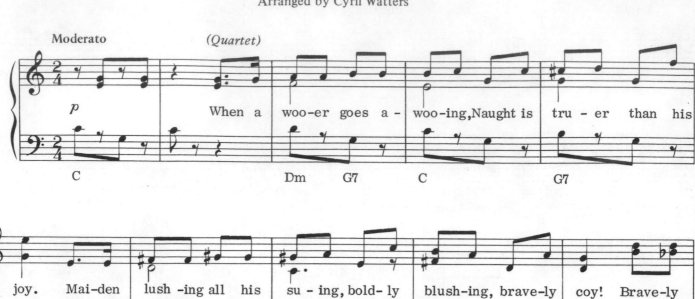

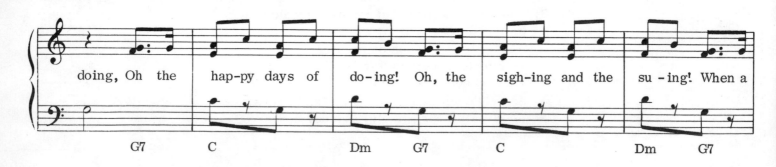

When a bro-ther leaves his sis-ter for an- oth -er, sis-ter weeps, Tears that

Cm   Fm6   G7   Cm E♭7

trick-le, tears that blis-ter, 'tis but mick-le sis - ter reaps! Tears that trick _____

A♭   D♭   E♭7   A♭   C7

_____ le, tears that blis _____ ter, Oh, the do - ing and un- doing, Oh, the

Fm   Fm6 G   G7

{ do - ing and un- do - ing, Oh, the sigh-ing and the su-ing, When a broth-er goes a -

 do - ing and un- do - ing, Oh, the sigh-ing and the su-ing, When a jest -er goes a -

C   Dm G7   C   Dm G7 C G7

To Coda ⊕

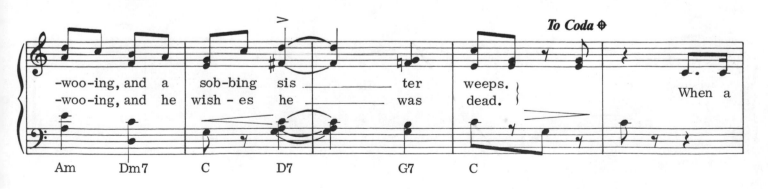

-woo-ing, and a sob-bing sis _____ ter weeps. }

-woo-ing, and he wish - es he _____ was dead. }

                   When a

Am Dm7 C D7   G7   C

23

Nothing Venture, Nothing Win

from Iolanthe

By Gilbert and Sullivan
Arranged by Cyril Watters

1. He____ who shies at such a prize is____ not
2. If you go in you're sure to win, Yours ____ will

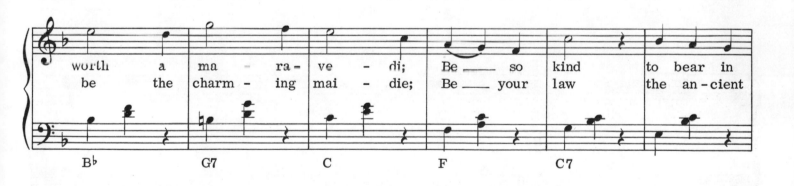

worth a ma - ra - ve - di; Be __ so kind to bear in
be the charm - ing mai - die; Be __ your law the an - cient

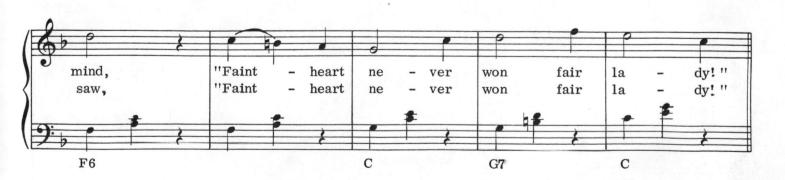

mind, "Faint - heart ne - ver won fair la - dy!"
saw, "Faint - heart ne - ver won fair la - dy!"

Strange Adventure

from The Yeoman Of The Guard

By Gilbert and Sullivan
Arranged by Cyril Watters

Tempo di Gavotte

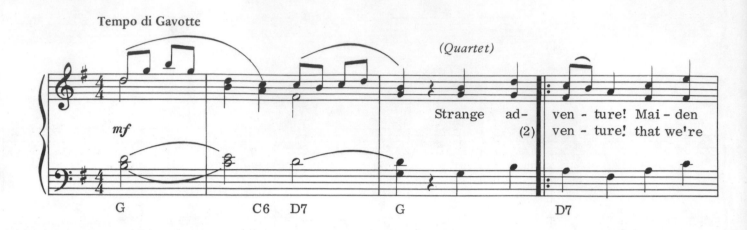

(Quartet)

Strange ad- ven - ture! Mai - den
(2) ven - ture! that we're

G   C6 D7   G   D7

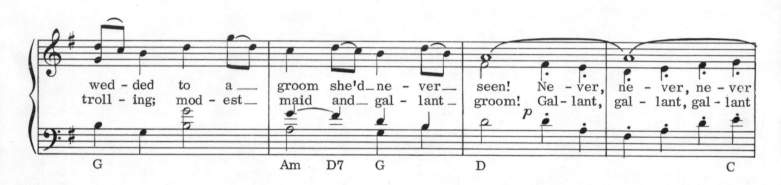

wed - ded   to   a ___ groom she'd ne - ver ___ seen!   Ne - ver,   ne - ver, ne - ver
troll - ing;   mod - est ___ maid   and   gal - lant ___ groom!   Gal - lant,   gal - lant, gal - lant

G   Am   D7   G   D   C

seen !   Groom a- bout ___ to   be   be- head - ed,   In   an ___ hour   on   Tow - er
groom!   While   the   fun' - ral   bell   is   toll - ing,   toll - ing, ___   toll - ing,   Bim - a -

D   A7   G   A7   D   G   Em   F#   Bm F# F#
                                                          (Bsus)

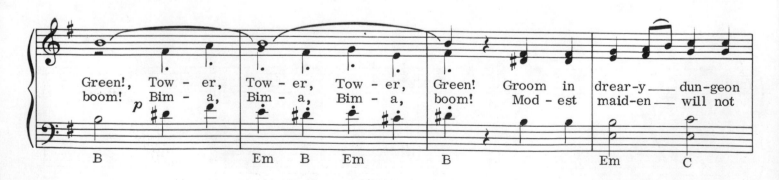

Green!,   Tow - er,   Tow - er,   Tow - er,   Green!   Groom   in   drear - y ___ dun-geon
boom!   Bim - a,   Bim - a,   Bim - a,   Bim - a,   boom!   Mod - est   maid - en ___ will not

B   Em   B   Em   B   Em   C

There Grew A Little Flower

from Ruddigore

By Gilbert and Sullivan
Arranged by Cyril Watters

Andante

(Hannah and Sir Roderick)

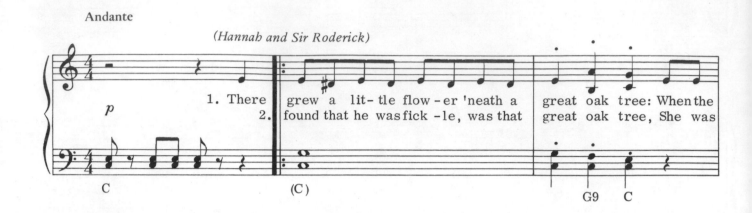

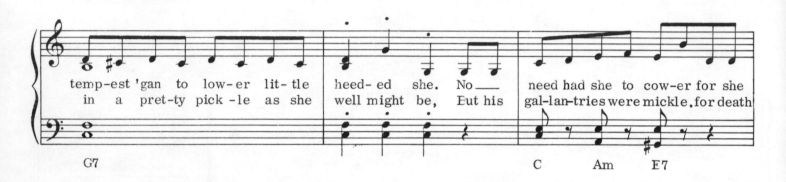

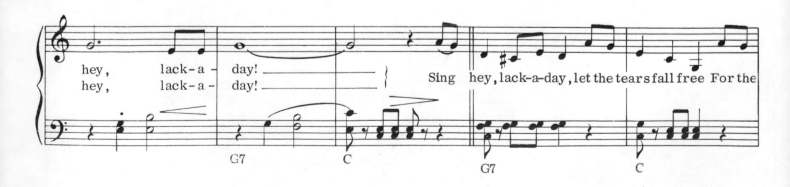

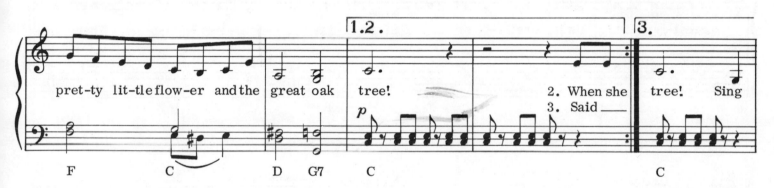

3. Said she " He loved me never, did that great oak tree,
    But I'm neither rich nor clever, and so why should he ?
    But though fate our fortunes sever, to be constant
                                            I'll endeavour,
    Aye, for ever and for ever, to my great oak tree'
    Sing hey, lack-a-day' etc.

He Is An Englishman

from H.M.S. Pinafore

By Gilbert and Sullivan
Arranged by Cyril Watters

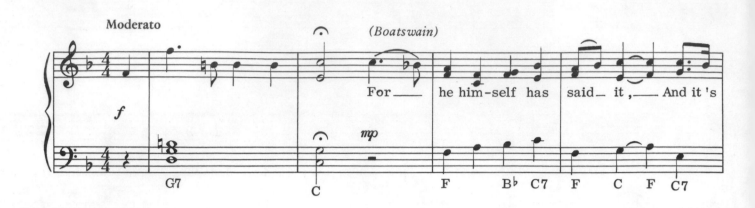

When A Merry Maiden Marries

from The Gondoliers

By Gilbert and Sullivan
Arranged by Cyril Watters

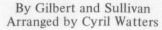

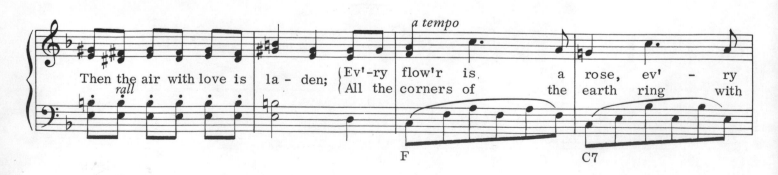

goose be-comes a | swan; Ev'-ry | kind of trou-ble | goes where the | last year's snows have
mu - sic sweet-ly | played, Wor-ry | is me-lo - dious | mirth, grief is | joy in mas-que-

F   C7   F   C7   F

gone! | Sun-light takes the place of | shade___ When you mar-ry, mer - ry | maid!___
-rade; | Sul -len night is laugh-ing | day,___ All the year is mer- ry | May!___

C7   F   C7   F   C7

1

When a mer - ry maid -en | mar - ries, | Sor-row goes and pleas-ure | tar - ries;
All the year is mer - ry | May,___ |

F   C7   F   C7

2

Ev'-ry sound be-comes a | song, All is | right and no-thing's | wrong. | All the year is mer-ry
rall. | *mp* | *a tempo* | | *ritard.*

F7   Bb   Ebm F   C7   F   F7

May! ___ Mer-ry, mer-ry May, mer-ry, mer-ry May, All the year is | mer-ry, mer - ry | May!
p a tempo | | | | *mf*

Bb Ebm F   C7   F   C7   F   G7   C7   F

35

I Have A Song To Sing, O!

from The Yeoman Of The Guard

By Gilbert and Sullivan
Arranged by Cyril Watters

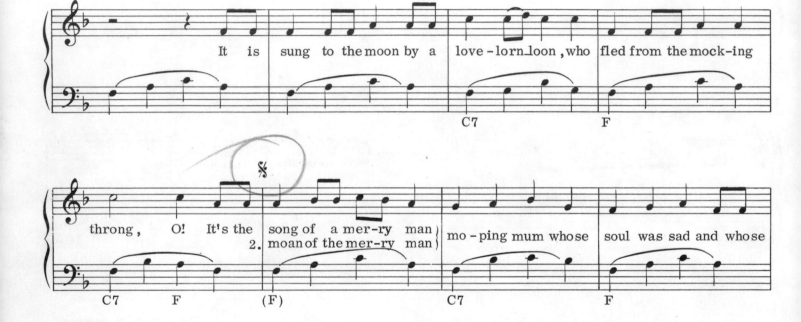

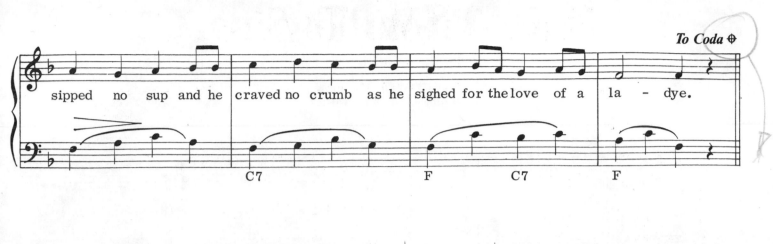

sipped no sup and he craved no crumb as he sighed for the love of a la - dye.

C7 · F · C7 · F

I have a song to sing O! What is your song, O! ____

mp

(No Chord) · B♭ · F · B♭ · F

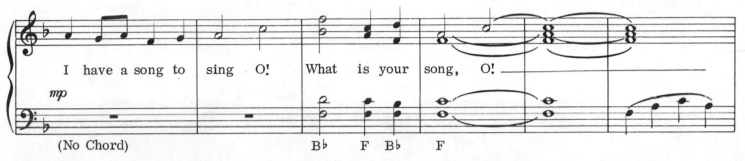

It is sung with the ring of the songs maids sing, who love with a love life-

C7 · F

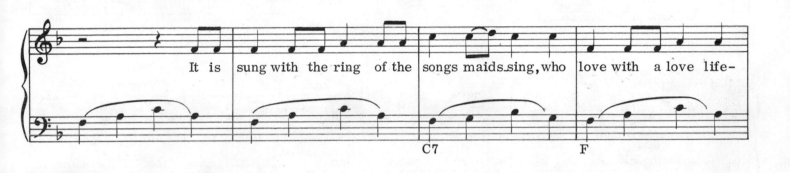

-long, O! It's the song of a mer-ry maid, nest-ling near, who loved her lord, but who

C7 · F · C7 · F

D. S. al Coda

dropped a tear at the

C7

⊕ *CODA*

mf

(No Chord) · F

Tit-Willow

from The Mikado

By Gilbert and Sullivan
Arranged by Cyril Watters

Three Little Maids From School

from The Mikado

By Gilbert and Sullivan
Arranged by Cyril Watters

Three lit-tle maids from school.   Three lit-tle maids who,

B   F#7   B   Bdim F#7   B   G7   C

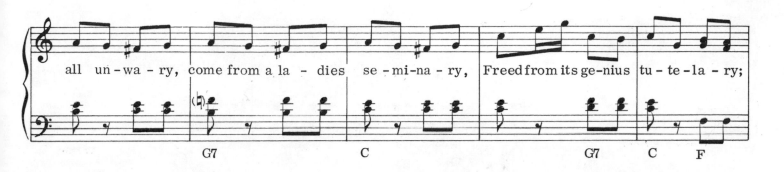

all un-wa-ry, come from a la - dies se-mi-na-ry, Freed from its ge-nius tu-te-la-ry;

                    G7   C   G7   C F

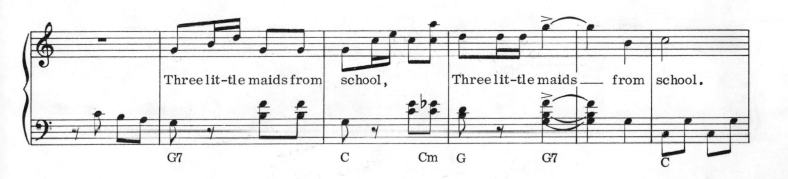

Three lit-tle maids from school,   Three lit-tle maids ___ from school.

G7   C   Cm G   G7   C

One lit-tle maid is a bride, Yum-Yum, Two lit-tle maids in at-ten-dance come,

E7   Am   E7   Am

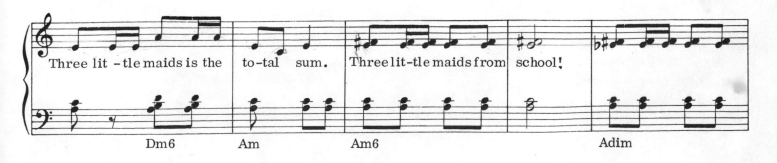

Three lit-tle maids is the to-tal sum. Three lit-tle maids from school!

Dm6   Am   Am6   Adim

From three lit-tle maids take one a-way, Two lit-tle maids re-main and they

Eb   Bb7   Eb   Bb7

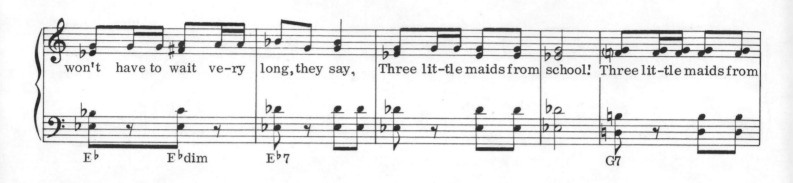

won't have to wait ve-ry long, they say, Three lit-tle maids from school! Three lit-tle maids from

Eb   Ebdim   Eb7   G7

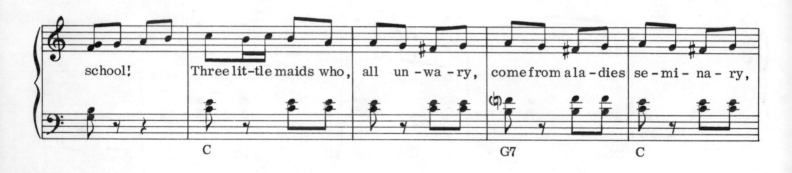

school!   Three lit-tle maids who, all un-wa-ry, come from a la-dies se-mi-na-ry,

C   G7   C

freed from its ge-nius tu-te-la-ry; Three lit-tle maids from school,

G7   C   F   G7   C   Cm

Three lit-tle maids____ from school!

G   G7   C   f   G7   C

Take A Pair of Sparkling Eyes

from The Gondoliers

By Gilbert and Sullivan
Arranged by Cyril Watters

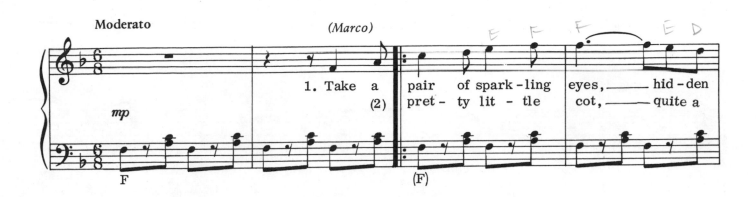

Prithee, Pretty Maiden

from Patience

By Gilbert and Sullivan
Arranged by Cyril Watters

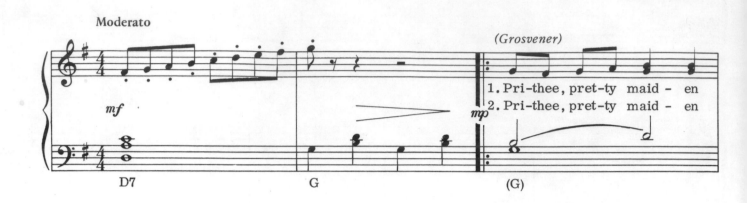

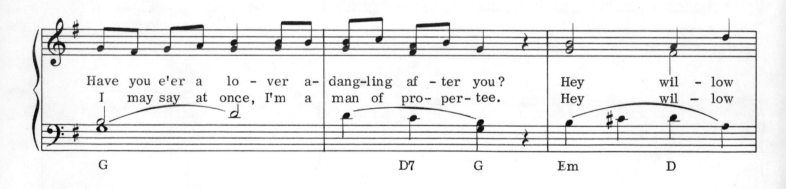